BM EDUCATION SERVICE LIBRARY

EARLY GOTHIC
ILLUMINATED
MANUSCRIPTS
IN ENGLAND

D1079833

EARLY GOTHIC ILLUMINATED MANUSCRIPTS IN ENGLAND

BY

D. H. TURNER

PUBLISHED BY
THE TRUSTEES OF
THE BRITISH MUSEUM
1969

© 1965, *The Trustees of the British Museum*

FIRST PUBLISHED 1965
REPRINTED 1969
SBN 7141 0437 X

11012

WITHDRAWN

BM12A (TUR)

PRINTED IN GREAT BRITAIN
AT THE UNIVERSITY PRESS, OXFORD
BY VIVIAN RIDLER
PRINTER TO THE UNIVERSITY

LIST OF ILLUSTRATIONS

Unless otherwise stated, references are to manuscripts
in the British Museum.

IN COLOUR

IN BLACK AND WHITE

(following page 22)

5

5. Matthew Paris, Virgin and Child. Royal MS. 14. C. vii, f. 6. *Circa* 1240–50

6. Matthew Paris, Lives of the Offas, Offa being armed as a knight. Cotton MS. Nero D. i, f. 3. *Circa* 1250

7. Westminster Psalter, St. Christopher. Royal MS. 2. A. xxii, f. 220^v. Mid-thirteenth century

8. Brother William, the Apocalyptic Christ. Cotton MS. Nero D. i, f. 156. Mid-thirteenth century

9. Trinity Apocalypse, the Adoration of Christ by the Four and Twenty Elders and the Marriage Supper of the Lamb. Trinity College, Cambridge, MS. R. 16. 2, f. 22. *Circa* 1245–50

10. Amesbury Psalter, the Crucifixion. All Souls College, Oxford, MS. 6, f. 5. Mid-thirteenth century

11. Apocalypse, the Woman drunk with the blood of the saints. Add. MS. 35166, f. 20^v. *Circa* 1260–70

12 Abingdon Apocalypse, St. John on the Isle of Patmos. Add. MS. 42555, f. 5. Before 1263

13. Oscott Psalter, upper roundel: the Adoration of Christ by the Magi; lower roundel: the Magi warned by an angel; mid-left: the Creator carrying the sleeping Adam; mid-right: the Creation of Eve. Add. MS. 50000, f. 9^v. *Circa* 1270

14. Douce Apocalypse, the Rider on the Red Horse. Bodleian Library, Oxford, MS. Douce 180, p. 14. Before 1272

15. Salvin Hours, the Tree of Jesse. Add. MS. 48985, f. 1^v. *Circa* 1275–80

16. Alphonso Psalter, Beatus page. Add. MS. 24686, f. 11. 1281–4

PREFACE

THIS BOOKLET describes and illustrates English illumination during a particular period of its history. The British Museum is fortunate in the possession of a fine collection of examples of the illumination to be discussed, including two of the best of them: the Evesham Psalter and the Oscott Psalter. In accordance with the purpose of the series of which the present booklet forms one, the illustrations in it have been drawn mainly from the Museum's holdings. It has, however, seemed desirable to include also reproductions from three manuscripts not in the Museum, namely the Trinity Apocalypse, the Amesbury Psalter, and the Douce Apocalypse. To their custiodans, the Master and Fellows of Trinity College, Cambridge, the Warden and Fellows of All Souls College, Oxford, and the Curators of the Bodleian Library, Oxford, grateful thanks are returned for permission to use the illustrations in question.

THE TERM GOTHIC IS NOW USUALLY APPLIED TO the art of the latter part of the Middle Ages in western Europe. The Gothic period starts some time in the thirteenth century and continues till some time in the fifteenth, that is until the Renaissance. Of course no hard and fast dates can be given to the beginning and end of the period and such limits as can be applied vary from country to country and region to region. Moreover, in any given region towards the beginning or end of a style there is overlapping with styles before or after it, and the production of works which are neither purely of the style in question nor purely of the one preceding or succeeding it. The history of art is not an exact science, and the student can at best only hope to chart the ebb and flow of various currents and seek to determine when a particular current dominates. Also—it will be obvious that a style lasting as long as the Gothic one did admits of various internal divisions. One such may be called the Early Gothic style, and it is with the illumination of books in this style in England that the present publication is concerned. Although only one branch of art, that of which we treat is a particularly important one, for, like all medieval illumination, it is the main source of information for the painting and drawing of its time and place. In the term Early Gothic I include not only the maturity of this first division of Gothic, but also the emergence and growth of the Gothic style in general. The period occupied by Early Gothic English illumination is some sixty to seventy years, or, more precisely, from about 1220 to 1285.

The year 1220 is a convenient one around which to start

our discussion. On Whitsunday 1220 the twelve-year-old King Henry III received his second and formal coronation, his first in 1216 having been a less splendid affair when the future was uncertain and civil war in the land. On Whitsun Eve 1220 the King had laid the foundation stone of a new Lady Chapel at Westminster Abbey, thus initiating that association with the abbey's rebuilding and embellishment for which he was to become so famed, and some weeks later he assisted at the translation of St. Thomas Becket to a new chapel in Canterbury Cathedral. Earlier in the same year the foundation stones had been laid for the new cathedral at Salisbury and the new west front at Wells Cathedral was apparently begun in the same twelvemonth.

The illumination of books in England *circa* 1220 is finely exampled in a group of manuscripts associated with the name of Robert de Lindesey, who was Abbot of Peterborough 1214–22. For him was apparently made a Psalter, now MS. 59[1] in the collection of the Society of Antiquaries of London which, according to liturgical evidence, is of the use of Peterborough Abbey. Its calendar includes mention of the Translation of Becket in the original hand so that the shortish time between that event and Abbot Robert's death is presumably that in which the book was written and decorated. Closely related to the Lindesey Psalter are another Psalter of the use of Peterborough, MS. 12, in the Fitzwilliam Museum at Cambridge,[2] and a fragment consisting of one leaf only added to the mid-eighth-century Psalter, Cotton MS. Vespasian A. i, in the British Museum. The British Museum leaf shows on one side a miniature of Christ in Majesty (Plate 1), and it and the main miniatures in the Lindesey and Fitzwilliam Psalters are all probably by one and the same hand.

The Lindesey group of illumination belongs less to the Gothic than to the so-called 'Transitional style', the style which comes between true Romanesque and Gothic, and

---

[1] E. G. Millar, *English Illuminated Manuscripts from the Xth to the XIIIth Century*, Paris and Brussels, 1926, pls. 69, 70.

[2] Ibid., pls. 71, 72; O. E. Saunders, *English Illumination*, ii, Florence and Paris, 1928, pls. 63, 64.

deserves treatment in its own right rather than just as an intermission. The Lindesey group is, however, late Transitional, containing several features which announce the advent of Gothic. The classicism and monumentality that are leading tendencies of the Transitional style are now tempered by a marked gracefulness and humanity, although we have the impression that these are a special effect rather than natural ingredients of the painting. Despite the clarity of execution in the Vespasian Christ and its simplified setting with the figures in the miniature standing out from the gold ground, as a whole the picture strikes us as rather posed and formal. Its colouring tends towards hardness and the major lines of composition are essentially hard and firm. This is still idealist art, not a representation in which we can share, and therefore not yet Gothic.

The liturgical indications in the Lindesey and Fitzwilliam Psalters point towards the monastery of Peterborough, but were they in fact made there ? All too little is known about the localization and working of ateliers of writing and illumination or the activities and movements of scribes and illuminators in our period for this question to be answered completely. The problems of when and whether illumination, especially illumination of high quality, is likely to be a 'home' or 'local', and a monastic rather than a secular product, have long aroused interest and do not often admit of ready solution. It has been suggested that already in the second quarter of the twelfth century the largest and most lavish manuscripts tended to be illuminated by professionals rather than monks.[1] In the thirteenth century the monasteries at St. Albans, Peterborough, and Canterbury probably had fairly flourishing and continuous ateliers of illumination, capable of work of good quality, but about other monastic centres we have less definite knowledge. Certainly the thirteenth century was that in which the professional scribe and illuminator and the stationer's guild, producing books to order, came into their own, and the finest books were more and more intended for personal rather than institutional use. The

[1] C. R. Dodwell, *The Great Lambeth Bible*, London, 1959, p. 18.

Lindesey group of illumination was probably executed at Peterborough, but it is worth recalling that the abbot after whom it is named also owned another Psalter, MS. D. 6, at St. John's College, Cambridge,[1] possibly produced in London, which contains illumination not belonging to the Lindesey group. This fact should help to prevent us taking too static a view of our subject.

Perhaps written and illuminated at Canterbury in the second quarter of the thirteenth century is a Bible, Burney MS. 3, in the British Museum,[2] which was owned by Robert de Bello, Abbot of St. Augustine's, Canterbury 1224–53. In size ($10\frac{1}{2} \times 7\frac{3}{4}$ inches) it is an example of the smallish, compact volume of the scriptures favoured in the thirteenth century, an age of keen biblical and theological studies. The various books of the bible are introduced by historiated initials of which that for Genesis (f. 10^v) is the most elaborate (Plate 2). In medallions down the shaft of the letter 'I' are scenes of the Creation, the bottom medallion showing the Trinity with the Father and Son side-by-side and the Holy Spirit as a dove, the tips of whose wings touch the mouths of the other two Persons. The story is continued in the decoration to the right where we see in medallions the Fall and Expulsion, Adam delving and Eve spinning, Noah's Ark, the Tower of Babel, and Abraham's sacrifice. The scenes in Robert de Bello's Bible are in the best tradition of narrative illustration. The figures are vivacious and lively, although the style of the illumination is rather linear and flat, therein resembling certain contemporary French work.

Related to the style of the Burney manuscript is that of the manuscripts associated with W. de Brailes,[3] in whom we may see a professional craftsman. He seems to have directed an atelier of illumination, the eight surviving manuscripts from which—two of them have his signature —though not entirely decorated by him, are all strongly

[1] Saunders, pl. 69.   [2] Saunders, pl. 75.
[3] S. C. Cockerell, *The Work of W. de Brailes*, Roxburghe Club, 1930; G. Pollard, 'William de Brailes', *The Bodleian Library Record*, v, Oxford, 1955, pp. 202–9.

influenced by him. He may well have been that William de Brailes who flourished from about 1230 to 1260, lived in Cat Street, Oxford, on the site of the present chapel of All Souls College, was a clerk in not more than minor orders, married to a wife Celena, and is known to have been in contact with illuminators. Two of the best products of the Brailes atelier are a Psalter, MS. 322 at New College, Oxford,[1] and a a Book of Hours, Add. MS. 49999 in the British Museum.[2] The latter, apparently the earliest existing separate English Book of Hours, is ornamented with eighteen large miniatures and eighty-eight historiated initials, all by Brailes himself. They contain scenes from the lives of Christ and the Virgin Mary, and such popular religious stories as that of Theophilus who sold himself to the Devil, the priest suspended from officiating by St. Thomas Becket, and the burgess who gave a chalice to a church of St. Laurence.

In Brailes we find not a great artist but a competent exponent of his craft, whose forte was his skill as a story-teller, at which he displays considerable originality. His scenes from the crucifixion in the British Museum Book of Hours (ff. 47^v, 48; Plate 3) lack the beauty to be found in the crucifixion miniatures in the Lindesey and Fitzwilliam Psalters, but they have a charm of their own, and the comparison just made is not a very fair one. The Lindesey and Fitzwilliam crucifixion miniatures are relatively large-scale works, already belonging to the tradition of independent picture-painting rather than just book-illustration. Brailes's crucifixion scenes are relatively small-scale and essentially book-illustration. Like all Brailes's miniatures they are expressive examples of narrative art, achieving a marked degree of characterization in the faces of the figures. Brailes included representations of himself in his work, such as that in MS. 330 in the Fitzwilliam Museum at Cambridge,[3] where, in the scene of the Last Judgement, he appears as a naked, tonsured man saved from hell by the intervention of St. Michael and accompanied by the

[1] Cockerell, pls. ii–xiii.
[2] Cockerell, pls. xviii–xx; Saunders, pl. 65a
[3] Cockerell, pls. xv–xvii; Millar, pl. 75.

legend: 'W. de Brail' me fecit.' His roots are firmly in the Transitional style, but there is about his work a naturalness, even rusticity, and the impression of a personal approach to his art, which are as evident in the minor forms of it, such as the decoration of margins or initials, as in its major forms, and are very Gothic in their appeal. An alliance of a keen interest in the narrative possibilities of art, such as we find in Brailes, with an appreciation of gracefulness and humanity, such as we found in the Lindesey group, played a large part in the genesis of English Gothic illumination.

There is something distinctly English about Brailes, although he is not without his points of contact with France. Certain manuscripts of English origin, however, survive from the mid-thirteenth century which are illuminated in a manner so close to that of certain French manuscripts, especially ones from the north-west of France, that they should be seen as the representatives on this side of the Channel of an 'Anglo-French' style. Such a manuscript is the Bible, Royal MS. I. D.i in the British Museum,[1] which contains a colophon to the effect that it was written by one William of Devon. Before the scriptures proper it has an illustration with scenes of the Coronation of the Virgin, the Crucifixion, and the Virgin and Child with Sts. Peter, Paul, and Martin (f. 4^v, Plate 4). In the bottom margin kneels a cleric, possibly the man for whom the book was made, who may perhaps be identified as Laurence de St. Martin, a royal clerk, who was Bishop of Rochester, 1251–74. The figural illumination in the Bible is in a flat, linear style with dull colours. Few folds disturb the draperies, and faces and hair are in a technique of outline drawing, with hardly any colour save touches of red on cheeks. It is a cold style, and the most lively features in the decoration of the Bible are the secondary motifs of grotesques and animals which inhabit its margins. Compared with the higher flights of Early Gothic painting in England and France the 'Anglo-French' style is provincial, standing apart from the main lines of development.

[1] Millar, pl. 77; Saunders, pl. 76.

If Brailes may be seen as a professional secular illuminator, Matthew Paris is the monastic craftsman *par excellence*. Born about the turn of the century, he took the habit of religion at St. Albans in 1217 and died there forty-two years later. According to a fourteenth-century account he was 'an eloquent and famous man . . . a magnificent historian and chronicler, an excellent author' and 'had such skill in the working of gold and silver and other metal and in painting pictures, that it is thought that there has been no equal to him since in the Latin world'.[1] Apart from a journey to Norway he is not known to have gone outside England, but he visited Westminster, Winchester, and Canterbury, and possibly York, and his acquaintances included the King, his brother the Earl of Cornwall and King of the Romans, the King of Norway, and other highly placed persons at home and abroad. We are not able to go so far in our appreciation of Matthew as the panegyrist quoted above, but in the history of art he has an abiding and merited distinction from the illumination executed or influenced by him.

The technique used by Matthew is one of outline drawing, and in him lives again the tradition of this kind of art which had had so distinguished a history in England going back to the Anglo-Saxon tenth century. Matthew's earlier works, like the illustrations to his *Lives of Sts. Alban and Amphibalus*, MS. E. I. 40 at Trinity College, Dublin,[2] which were probably done before 1240, show already a mastery of the use of line which never left him and was his prime characteristic. He excelled especially at contrasts between lighter inner lines and stronger outer ones, and there is a definite attempt to imply the rounded form beneath draperies. Colour he employed only in tinting or shading, as a secondary component of his art, an ornamental finish to it. Despite his renown, however, he is not a highly original or forward-looking artist. He looks back to the Transitional

---

[1] *Chronica S. Albani: Gesta Abbatum*, i, Rolls Series, xxviii. 4, 1867, p. 395.

[2] Facsimile reproduction: W. R. Lowe and E. F. Jacob, *Illustrations to the Life of St. Alban*, Oxford, 1924; Millar, pl. 89*a*.

style and its classical revival, and as he grew older his own style grew more and more firm and monumental. In the signed drawing of the Virgin and Child with himself at their feet in the British Museum, Royal MS. 14 C. vii, f. 6 (Plate 5), probably executed *circa* 1240–50, he uses more colour than usual, not with altogether happy effect. The picture's outlines are so thick and strong and some of its details so solid and heavy that if they are to support more colour than the merest tinting it should be full colour. The best parts of the miniature are the faces of the Virgin and Child with their tender dignity. In them we feel we are looking at something verging on a human relationship rather than a hieratic idealization. In general though the miniature tends to formality, with the statuesque and imposing figure of the Virgin dominating over the crouching Matthew, who does not even look up at them. They are as it were an over-powering vision in his mind rather than a representation at which he is actually looking. The style of the miniature is not quite Gothic, but it is as Gothic as it could be from a conservative like its author.

No discussion of Matthew Paris can omit the marginal drawings which illustrate his historical writings. The most important of these is the *Chronica Majora*, the first two volumes of the original manuscript of which are in MSS. 26 and 16 at Corpus Christi College, Cambridge, the third is in Royal MS. 14 C. vii in the British Museum. The Chronicle goes down to 1259, and the writing of it was commenced before 1245. Not all its marginal drawings are by Matthew himself but all were presumably produced under his direction. Many events are commented on only in sign language, and the choice of what to illustrate and the degree of completeness to give to the treatment of it were governed by Matthew's insatiable curiosity and his feeling for the sensational and anecdotal more than by any ideas of relative importance. As examples of his tendencies may be cited the seven drawings dealing with Earl Richard of Cornwall's journey to the Holy Land in 1240–2, including one of the two Saracen girls walking on balls of metal whom the Earl saw at the court of the Emperor Frederick II in Sicily

I. Evesham Psalter, the Crucifixion. *Circa* 1250-60

II. Evesham Psalter, Beatus page. *Circa* 1250–60

(Corpus Christi MS. 16, f. 149), and another of the elephant carrying a band of musicians on a wooden platform which was a feature of the Earl's reception at Cremona (ibid., f. 151ᵛ). The representations of the Wandering Jew (ibid., f. 70ᵛ)[1] and a 'Maiden in Burgundy molested by a Young Man' (ibid., f. 61ᵛ) are good instances of Matthew's ability to convey the mood of an incident.

The later stage of Matthew Paris's style is best seen in his illustrations to his *The Lives of the Offas* in Cotton MS. Nero D. i in the British Museum[2] (Plate 6). The text of the *Lives* was not finished before 1250, and the first five illustrations, which are the only ones completed by Matthew himself, are presumably of about this date. They are virtually without colour so that the basic linearism of the style is emphasized. The softer and lighter touch of the younger man who was responsible for the illustrations to the *Lives of Sts. Alban and Amphibalus* has now become a strong and vigorous handling of line. Drapery folds are moving towards a particular kind of Gothic multiplication and complication, which will be our concern shortly, but Matthew has them firmly under control. By no means insensitive to the newer, Gothic trends in art, he does not allow himself to be carried away by them, fitting them, in so far as he accepts them, into his own well-established style. Yet the debt that English art owes to Matthew Paris should not be belittled. The reincarnation in him of the tradition of outline drawing and the heights to which he raised it did a great deal to inspire and make possible the subsequent successes of Early Gothic illumination in England.

What could be built on the foundation laid by Matthew is seen in five tinted drawings added to the Westminster Psalter, which was originally executed *circa* 1200 and is Royal MS. 2 A. xxii in the British Museum.[3] They may be regarded as by a more forward looking and younger follower of Matthew, and dated to the mid-thirteenth century. The drawing of St. Christopher with the Christ

---

[1] P. Brieger, *English Art 1216–1307*. The Oxford History of English Art, iv, 1957, pl. 46*a*.   [2] Millar, pl. 88; Saunders, pls. 81, 82.
[3] Millar, pl. 90; Saunders, pl. 85.

Child (f. 220ᵛ; Plate 7) inevitably invites comparison with Matthew's Virgin and Child. Like it the St. Christopher, and the other added drawings in the Westminster Psalter, are in the tradition of independent picture painting. In every respect the St. Christopher is an advance on the Virgin and Child. The absence not only of a background but also of a frame gives a greater illusion of surrounding space to the figures. The monumentality and formality of the Virgin and Child are replaced by naturalness and plasticity. Despite the broad way in which the subject is treated and the thickness of the outlines its artist gives to the miniature a touching gentleness and grace. Because of this, because we could identify ourselves with Christopher and sympathize with his expression as he attempts to carry the Desire of the World, we can say that what we are looking at is a true Gothic picture. In it the humanizing spirit of the thirteenth century, exemplified in the life of St. Francis and in legends like that of St. Anthony of Padua receiving the Christ Child into his arms, is realized in art.

Matthew Paris is familiar for his disapproval of the new religious orders of friars which appeared in the thirteenth century. He recognized, however, the sanctity of individual Franciscans and the learning of individual Dominicans. He even went so far as to insert into his *Liber Additamentorum*, now in Cotton MS. Nero D. i. in the British Museum, a drawing of the Apocalyptic Christ (f. 156, Plate 8), with a statement attributing it to 'Brother William of the Order of Minors, a companion of the blessed Francis, second in the same order, holy in life, by nation an Englishman'. This appears to be a Brother William the Englishman who is mentioned in some early Franciscan records as a companion of Francis, near whom he was buried at Assisi. He seems to have lived at least until 1239, but where or when he executed the drawing of Christ, or how it came to St. Albans cannot be ascertained. It is a noble and impressive work, calm and dignified more than emotional and humanizing. The product obviously of a deeply religious mind, it is distinctly statuesque and less Gothic than the drawing of St. Christopher which we examined previously, and which seems to reflect better the joyous spirit of the founder of the Franciscans. On the back of Brother William's miniature is a note 'let nothing more be written on this page lest the picture be damaged, because the parchment is transparent, and it can be seen better if held up to the light', the latter part of which advice can be proved by practice, when the artistic prowess of Brother William will be all the more appreciated.

Mention of a representation of Christ as he appeared to the author of the Apocalypse brings us to a special phenomenon of our period, namely the production of illustrated manuscripts of the Apocalypse, of which no less than eighteen of probable origin in England in the thirteenth century survive. The apocalyptic vein seems to have been one to which the times were sympathetic and in the twelfth to thirteenth centuries the Revelation of St. John was being interpreted in a new, optimistic spirit in the light of history, as in the commentaries on it of Joachim of Flora and Alexander of Bremen. Foremost of the English illustrated Apocalypses is MS. R. 16. 2 in the library of Trinity College, Cambridge.[1] Not all its miniatures seem to have been part of the book's original decoration, and those that were are divisible into two groups, each by a different artist, one of whom is superior to the other and the dominant and more important personality in the illumination of the manuscript. His work (Plate 9) is in a technique, in which, despite the amount of colour employed on occasion, the drawing is more important than the colouring. It is thereby closer to the techniques of Matthew Paris or the miniatures added to the Westminster Psalter than to true full-colour painting, in which the colouring and the drawing may be of equal importance or the colouring all important.

However, our Trinity artist was certainly not without skill in the use of colour. His contrasts between lighter and darker shades and virtual absences of colour are very effective, but his most interesting characteristic and his most valuable contribution to artistic development is his treatment of draperies. These have thick, rope-like folds, which

[1] Facsimile reproduction: M. R. James, *The Trinity Apocalypse*, Roxburghe Club, 1909; Millar, pls. 85, 86; Saunders, pls. 92, 93.

19

sometimes nearly cover the surfaces at their disposal, at others leave flat oval patches on them, especially around and over muscles and joints. There is thus a strong contrast between the flat, regularly patterned and designed grounds of the miniatures and the irregular, disturbed draperies of the figures in them. The result may be artificial rather than natural, but it creates a strong impression of richness and vigour. Faces are less successful, being round, rather large, and often with over-emphasized jaws. They tend to have fixed, staring expressions, not infrequently with an air of surprise or bewilderment, as on the face of the Bride embracing the Lamb in our illustration.

The original writing and illumination of the Trinity Apocalypse have been variously dated between 1230 and 1250, and for the place of origin of the manuscript St. Albans, Westminster, and Salisbury have been suggested. The better group of its original miniatures are in an individual and striking style, which for convenience will henceforth be referred to as 'the Trinity Apocalypse style', and which marks a new departure in English illumination. It has two main lines of descent. One leads to Matthew Paris and is represented primarily in the treatment of faces, but also in the strong outlines. In these respects there does seem to be a direct relationship with Matthew, and in particular with his later period as instanced in the *Lives of the Offas*. The other line of descent is that represented in the treatment of draperies and it does not seem to lead to obvious English origins. It stems from the kind of classicizing drapery found in the earlier thirteenth century in sculpture and illumination in the North French and Rhenish regions as in the famous Ingeburg Psalter, MS. 1695, in the Musée Condé at Chantilly.[1] In English sculpture it appears around 1240–5. Stylistic evidence in fact suggests that the original work on the Trinity Apocalypse was done *circa* 1245–50 and the Abbey of St. Albans is the only place which can put forward a real claim to being the site of it.

[1] J. Porcher, *French Miniatures from Illuminated Manuscripts*, London, 1960, pl. xli. There is a set of photographs of the manuscript kept as Facsimile 277 in the Department of Manuscripts at the British Museum.

The further development of the Trinity Apocalypse style is found in another Apocalypse, MS. fr. 403, in the Bibliothèque Nationale, Paris,[1] and the Evesham Psalter, Add. MS. 44874, in the British Museum. These two manuscripts must be very close to each other in date, and probably have at least one artist in common. The Paris Apocalypse is illustrated in tinted outline on plain backgrounds in a softer and more fluid style than that of the Trinity Apocalypse. Drapery folds are less regular and more broken, and expressions on faces less fixed. The Evesham Psalter can be dated on liturgical evidence after 1246, and was apparently intended for an Abbot of Evesham, although whether it was executed there cannot be decided for certain. Of its crucifixion miniature (f. 6; Colour plate I) it has been rightly said that it reaches the high-water mark of English illumination of its period. At some time in the thirteenth century the Psalter seems to have come into the possession of Earl Richard of Cornwall, and this may have been after the Battle of Evesham in 1265, when the abbey, which had given burial to Simon de Montfort who fell in the battle and was regarded as an arch-traitor in Royalist eyes, may have wanted to placate the Court.

The Evesham Psalter contains figural illumination in two techniques: full-colour and shaded drawing on colour ground. Two artists were probably responsible for this illumination, the second being a follower of the first. The second hand may be seen in the Beatus page of the manuscript, that is to say the page with the initial 'B' to Psalm i (f. 7ᵛ; Colour plate II). This is a fine example of such a page from our period. It is in full colour and shows a balanced design, in which the basic feature—the initial—is well preserved and emphasized. By the major artist of the Psalter is the miniature of the Crucifixion (Colour plate I) which is one of the masterpieces of English medieval art. The secrets of its success are its subtle composition and expert contrasts, which can all be traced back to the Trinity Apocalypse style, compared with which, however, great

[1] Facsimile reproduction: L. Delisle and P. Meyer, *L'Apocalypse en français au XIII° siècle*, Paris, 1901; Millar, pl. 91; Saunders, pl. 90

progress has been made. The Trinity style had something unresolved and experimental about it, what we are dealing with now is assured and practised. The faces of Christ, Mary, and John show real emotion, and we may notice especially the positioning of Mary and John—how the way in which they overlap the frame of the miniature and the coloured grounds behind them, combined with their dramatic and contorted poses, places them in planes in front of and really diagonal to the cross, on to which attention is thereby directed. They look down at the abbot, who does not crouch outside the miniature proper as did Matthew Paris before his Virgin and Child, but reaches up into it. Mary and John are truly intermediary between God and man, and there is in this picture a real link between the divine and the human, the eternal and the temporal.

The achievement in the Evesham Crucifixion is even more apparent if it is compared with the corresponding miniature in a Psalter made for a nun of the Abbey of Amesbury, MS. 6 at All Souls College, Oxford[1] (f. 5 ; Plate 10). The Amesbury Psalter is one of a group of manuscripts associated with the scriptorium of the Cathedral of Salisbury and the directing personality in their illumination is known as 'the Sarum illuminator'.[2] The British Museum possesses only one member of the group, a Bible, Royal MS. I B. xii, written in 1254 by a William de Hales for Thomas de la Wile, who had been put in charge of the schools at Salisbury. Like all the work of the Sarum illuminator the miniatures in the Amesbury Psalter are very accomplished, firm and balanced in execution, strong and rich in colouring, but in general their style is rather hard and formal. Their author must have been in contact with the stylistic group formed by the Trinity and Paris Apocalypses and the Evesham Psalter but his products do not belong to it. He is more traditional, and though in one set of miniatures, namely those in the Missal of Henry of Chichester, MS. lat. 24 in the John Rylands Library, Man-

[1] Millar, pls. 81–83 ; Saunders, pls. 85b, 86.
[2] A. Hollaender, 'The Sarum Illuminator and his School', *Wiltshire Archaeological and Natural History Magazine*, i, 1942–4, pp. 230–62.

chester,[1] he worked in a true Gothic idiom, he does not quite do so in the Amesbury Psalter. Iconographically its Crucifixion miniature is very close to the Evesham Crucifixion, but it does not evoke that personal response that the other does. It does not show to the same degree as the Evesham Crucifixion that prime concern of the Early Gothic artist, which was to increase the viewer's share in what was being portrayed. The realization of this end meant that art became increasingly representational and naturalistic, for its intention was to provide something which could be seen as an extension, at its highest a sublimation of the viewer's own life. This the Evesham Crucifixion does, for it manages to present its subject as an eternal event happening before our eyes as we look at it. The resultant emotional effect is one of the hall-marks of Early Gothic, and the Evesham Crucifixion miniature is the fullest first manifestation of the Early Gothic style in English illumination.

Related in some ways to the Sarum group of illumination and also to the group to which the Evesham Psalter belongs, but standing apart from both, is a mid-thirteenth-century Psalter in the collection of the Duke of Rutland at Belvoir Castle.[2] Its provenance is unknown, but it may have connexions with Edmund de Lacey, Earl of Lincoln (d. 1258). The marginal decoration of the book abounds in grotesques, and its miniatures are executed in a sharper and more virile manner than those in the Sarum group, having certain pecularities such as white hatching on garments. They begin to show traces of a process of maturing and consolidation which English Early Gothic illumination underwent in the third quarter of the thirteenth century. In such a manuscript as the *Life of St. Edward the Confessor*, MS. Ee. 3. 59 in the University Library, Cambridge,[3] this process can be seen at work within the covers of one book. The Cambridge Life of St. Edward may be considered a copy of an original illustrated *Life* (now lost) by Matthew Paris,

[1] Millar, pl. 84; Saunders, pls. 67, 68.

[2] Facsimile reproduction: E. G. Millar, *The Rutland Psalter*, Roxburghe Club, 1937; Millar, *English Illuminated Manuscripts*, pls. 78–80.

[3] Facsimile reproduction: M. R. James, *La Estoire de St Aedward le Rei*, Roxburghe Club, 1920; Millar, pl. 89*b*; Saunders, pls. 83, 84.

the influence of whom is discernible throughout its miniatures. The earlier of these are also influenced by the Trinity Apocalypse style, from which the later move away towards something quieter and more regularized.

In the British Museum an Apocalypse, Add. MS. 35166 (Plate 11),[1] provides early examples of the maturing of English Gothic illumination. The book has a sister-manuscript, formerly numbered 10 in the collection of C. W. Dyson Perrins at Malvern.[2] In both Apocalypses the illustrations are in a basically outline technique on plain backgrounds, but colouring is getting stronger and flatter and is so extensively applied on occasion that the outline technique is transformed into one of painting. The derivation of the style in the two Apocalypses from that of the Trinity Apocalypse is obvious. Signs of the times, however, are that the lines of drapery are tending to straighten and folds to deepen. Faces are lengthening, with cheeks hollowing and foreheads broadening, and the resultant type is one which will be a characteristic of English painting *circa* 1270. The miniatures retain a considerable delicacy and freshness and many scenes are particularly vivid as can be seen from our illustration of St. John's vision of the woman drunk with the blood of the saints from the British Museum Apocalypse. The corresponding miniature in the Dyson Perrins Apocalypse shows a thoroughly Bacchanalian drunkard.

Heavier colouring and less elegant draughtsmanship are found in another pair of Apocalypses, one of which again is in the British Museum. They are the former MS. 55 in the collection of Henry Yates Thompson, which passed to C. S. Gulbenkian in 1920,[3] and Add. MS. 42555 in the Museum (Plate 12). This was given to the Abbey of Abingdon by Giles Bridport, Bishop of Salisbury from 1257 till his death in 1263. The Gulbenkian Apocalypse and it have close relations with another Apocalypse, MS. 209 in the library

[1] Millar, pl. 92; Saunders, pls. 94, 95a.

[2] Facsimile reproduction: M. R. James, *The Apocalypse in Latin*, Oxford, 1927; Saunders, pl. 95b.

[3] Photographs of the manuscript are Facsimile 560 (1) in the Department of Manuscripts at the British Museum.

of Lambeth Palace,[1] which was possibly commissioned by Eleanor, the third wife of Roger de Quincy, Earl of Winchester (d. 1264), who subsequently married Sir Roger Leyburn, a personal friend of King Edward I. It has been suggested that the de Quincy, Abingdon, and Gulbenkian Apocalypses were produced at the Abbey of St. Augustine's, Canterbury, but the evidence for this attribution is not over convincing. The illumination of both the Abingdon and Gulbenkian books was unfinished originally, and their standard is lower than that of the two Apocalypses we discussed in the previous paragraph. The draperies in them are ample and loose, with very deep folds, more what we normally think of when we speak of a Gothic fold. Backgrounds are coloured and patterned and compositions rather awkward. Faces are lengthened and cheeks hollowed so much that at times they reach the point of malformation, indeed the expressions on them are often grotesque or little better than caricatures. In general the style is rough and the colouring smudgy, and there is an atmosphere of violence and even ugliness about the illustrations.

The two finest illuminated manuscripts of the Early Gothic period in England in its maturity after the extravagant flourish of youth which we saw in the miniature of the Crucifixion in the Evesham Psalter, are the Oscott Psalter and the Douce Apocalypse. The Oscott Psalter is now Add. MS. 50000 in the British Museum[2] and owes its name to having been at St. Mary's College, Oscott, in the nineteenth to twentieth centuries. Its original provenance and destination have not been determined, but it includes a calendar, which though definitely for English use, has noticeable French and possibly Italian interests as well. The nature and quality of the Psalter certainly suggest it was made for a person rather than a place. It is throughout a very sophisticated product, a typical page of its text, with its elaborately flourished initials, its line-endings, and its animals and grotesques in the margin, making a similar page of the Evesham Psalter appear almost archaic by comparison.

[1] Saunders, pls. 71–74, 98.   [2] Saunders, pl. 70.

25

The chief glory of the Oscott Psalter, however, is its series of twenty-two full-page miniatures. Ten of these show single figures of saints (Colour plates III and IV), and the remainder have scenes of the Life of Christ (Plate 13), the Last Judgement, Christ in Majesty, and King David. At least four miniatures are missing and the single saints were probably meant for the Twelve Apostles and will be taken as such now. They and the representation of King David seem to be by another and better artist than the one responsible for the rest of the full-page miniatures. The artist of the Apostles delights in broad expanses of colour such as can be seen in his backgrounds and on the draperies of his figures. On flesh he uses only slight modelling, and hair is in an outline technique. For tunics he prefers a flattish treatment with gold. There is thus a contrast between the bodies and under-garments of his figures and their softer mantles with their sweeping lines and deeper folds. The techniques used in the Oscott Apostles represent a refinement of those used in the Trinity Apocalypse and the Evesham Psalter and back to the style of these books too stems the manner of presentation of the Oscott Apostles. Essentially it is a dramatic presentation. The Apostles are not taking part in actual scenes, but they are by no means hieratic icons. With their swaying postures and their positioning on the threshold of their enclosures, their concerned expressions and gesticulating fingers, they are living figures taking part in some sort of action or dialogue. This is not a dialogue with the occupant of the facing miniature, as can be seen from the manuscript, but an action of which the Apostles are the only visible part, the remainder being implied.

The saint in the first of our colour plates from the Oscott Psalter has no attribute to identify him, but he recalls the type of St. John the Evangelist that we found in the Evesham and Amesbury Psalters. The saint in the second colour plate is Bartholomew, and he is shown holding his own skin, which was flayed off him at his martyrdom, and the knife used for the operation. His contorted posture is a carrying to extreme of the kind of posture in which St. John appeared in the two manuscripts just mentioned. All the artists we have considered so far were either primarily draughtsmen or as much draughtsmen as painters—and in some illumination we may have been looking at drawing by one man and colouring by another—but the artist of the Oscott Apostles is primarily a painter and it is no wonder his work has been compared to wall or panel paintings. A relationship has been proposed between it and the paintings on the ceiling of the Chapter House at Christ Church, Oxford, but this does not seem to be valid. Its nearest relatives in fact are the paintings on the so-called Retable in Westminster Abbey, which were probably executed about 1270. However, even when allowance is made for the difference in media, the style of the Westminster Retable is still more painterly and advanced than that of the Oscott Apostles.

The original arrangement of the full-page miniatures in the Oscott Psalter was that they formed a series of diptychs in which two pages of scenes from the Life of Christ normally alternated with two Apostles, the latter being as it were on the outside leaves of the diptychs. This scheme betrays French influence, as does the presentation of the scenes from the Life of Christ, two to a page within roundels or medallions and with supplementary scenes in part roundels in the corners and at the sides of the miniatures (Plate 13). It is in the illustrated *Bibles moralisées* produced in France in the mid-thirteenth century that we particularly find such a method of presentation and it derives from the techniques of stained-glass windows. The scenes from the Life of Christ in the Oscott Psalter are in a more linear and less expert style than the miniatures of the Apostles. Faces have less colour in their modelling and their pronounced elongation and the chevron-markings that occur on foreheads are definitely manneristic.

Closer to the Westminster Retable than the Oscott Psalter is the Douce Apocalypse, MS. Douce 180 in the Bodleian Library, Oxford[1] (Plate 14). The arms born by

---

[1] Facsimile reproduction: M. R. James, *The Douce Apocalypse*, Roxburghe Club, 1922; A. G. and W. O. Hassall, *The Douce Apocalypse*, London, 1961; Millar, pls. 93, 94; Saunders, pl. 97*b*.

the man and woman in the initial at the beginning of its text suggest it was made for Edward I and his wife Eleanor of Castille before their accession to the throne in 1272. The Apocalypse's illustrations are unfinished and show work in various stages of completion, that without colour allowing us to appreciate the more the artist's excellent draughtsmanship and composition. The miniatures are carefully designed with admirable attention to the counterpoise of their contents and the directions in which the viewer's eye is to be led. In our reproduction of the miniature of St. John's vision of the Rider on the Red Horse there is a circular progression which starts with the ox and leads round through St. John to the Rider and up again to the Lamb. Out of this circle the Rider bursts at a tangent. His diagonal lines of progression—the main one of his horse and the secondary one of his cloak—are counter-balanced by the vertical lines on the left of the picture—the main one of the apostle and the secondary one of the tree.

The artist of the Douce Apocalypse was as expert in the use of colour as he was in the use of line. In our illustration he subtly blends shades of blue and green with ones of red and brown and the strongest tones are given to the cloak of the Rider which is a deep, rich red lined with vair. It thereby becomes a central feature of the picture and the impression of dramatic speed which it emphasizes, both in colouring and drawing, leaves us in no doubt of the effect of the Rider's mission to take peace from the earth. The naturalistic leaves on the tree in the miniature and the outsize, naturalistic grasses on the ground are an interesting feature of the Douce Apocalypse. Drapery and faces develop further the tendencies we have noticed in English Early Gothic illumination in its maturer phase, and hair is noticeably in a crisp, formalized manner. Resemblances have been remarked upon between the Douce Apocalypse and the Cambridge copy of Matthew Paris's *Life of St. Edward,* which we discussed earlier. It is indeed the style of the Cambridge manuscript which stands at the beginning of the development leading to the Oscott Psalter and the Douce Apocalypse. Matthew Paris's original manuscript of

the *Life of St. Edward* may well have been given to the
Queen, Eleanor of Provence, to whom it was dedicated,
and it therefore becomes more than a probability that the
copy of it was made in an atelier of book-production
attached to the royal Court. In view of its associations the
Douce Apocalypse may also be credited to such an atelier.
About the Oscott Psalter we can be less sure, but on stylistic
grounds we may consider the Douce Apocalypse and it as
representatives of a 'Court' tradition of illumination. The
date of both manuscripts is likely to be about 1270.

A more provincial tradition is found in two books associated with the diocese of Lincoln, which are apparently
from one and the same atelier. They are the Salvin Hours,
Add. MS. 48985 in the British Museum[1] (Plate 15), and the
Huth Psalter, Add. MS. 38116 in the British Museum.[2] The
former is so called because it belonged from at least the
late seventeenth century to 1904 to the Salvin family of
Durham, the latter was part of a bequest to the Museum by
Alfred H. Huth, who died in 1910. Its calendar includes the
feast of the Translation of St. Hugh, Bishop of Lincoln,
which took place in 1280. The Salvin Hours was perhaps
executed a little before this date. The prevalent style of the
miniatures in both manuscripts is flat and dry, with rather
cold colours, although the first of the two artists in the
Salvin Hours, who was responsible for the initial containing
a Tree of Jesse (f. 1ᵛ) in our illustration, rises above these
limitations. In both its figural and its purely decorative
illumination the Salvin Hours has many features recalling
the style of W. de Brailes. Such are the expressions on the
faces of the figures in the Tree of Jesse, or the elongated
dragons with foliate tails and the scrolls on rectangular
panels with gable-like projections which occur in the
margins. Its decorated initials are in fact more Romanesque
than Gothic with their ornamental foliage inhabited by
clambering and contorted animals and humans. If the
Oxford localization of Brailes's atelier be accepted, then
Oxford, which was in the diocese of Lincoln, would similarly

[1] Millar, pls. 97, 98.
[2] Saunders, pl. 88.

29

be a very good place to which to assign the execution of the Salvin Hours in view of its connexion with Brailes's work. Its miniatures and those in the Huth Psalter also seem to have relations with those in the Bible of William of Devon, which we discussed earlier.

In the latter part of the Early Gothic period the best illumination is associated with the royal Court rather than provincial centres like St. Albans or Peterborough. We saw this with the Douce Apocalypse and the Oscott Psalter and we find it again in the 1280's with the Alphonso Psalter and the Ashridge College *Petrus Comestor: Historia Scholastica*. The latter is Royal MS. 3 D. vi in the British Museum[1] and was presented by Earl Edmund of Cornwall (d. 1300) to Ashridge College in Buckinghamshire, which he founded in 1283. The former is Add. MS. 24686 in the British Museum[2] (Plate 16) and was apparently begun not earlier than 1281 in connexion with a projected marriage of Prince Alphonso, then eldest son of King Edward I, to Margaret, daughter of the Count of Holland. The illumination of the manuscript was only partly completed originally, presumably because of the Prince's death in 1284. It is in a style close to that of the *Petrus Comestor* and which is a later version of that of the Douce Apocalypse. Both the psalter and the *Petrus Comestor* books make frequent use of naturalistic and heraldic motifs in their decoration. Such will be noticed in our illustration of the Beatus page from the Psalter (f. 11), which is part of the manuscript's original illumination, where a heron, a bullfinch, a kingfisher, and a gull can be recognized in the margins. In general the illumination is taking on an appearance of lavishness and luxuriousness, qualities which will be dominant ones in the succeeding—the 'East Anglian'—artistic period. It is also becoming conventionalized and standardized. With this decline into mannerism we draw to the end of the Early Gothic period in English illumination. Indeed the Alphonso Psalter and the *Petrus Comestor* are transitional works, belonging as much to the 'East Anglian' style as the one before it.

[1] Millar, pl. 95; Saunders, pls. 77, 78.
[2] Millar, pl. 96; Saunders, pls. 86, 87.

In the period we have reviewed the true examples of Early Gothic illumination in England had about them the vigour and freshness of a new style and one that was closer in ideals and inspiration to ordinary human life than the Romanesque style had been. By comparison with English Romanesque art English Gothic has on occasion been disparaged. With this judgement in so far as it applies to illumination in the first period of Gothic the present writer finds himself in disagreement. It is true that in the limited field of pure book illustration the best Early Gothic work is probably that done in Paris, such as the Psalter of St. Louis, MS. lat. 10525 in the Bibliothèque Nationale, Paris.[1] Here is an aristocratic elegance which we do not find in England, but towards which English illumination increasingly aspired after about 1260. Yet the French work is never more than book illustration. Its English counterpart moved in a different mode. At its best it is independent painting or drawing in its own right and even in its lesser examples there is a freedom of spirit not seen in France. More and more in England the page rather than the whole book was becoming the measure and object of illumination, and there was an infiltration of the monumental art of the fresco into the art of the book. In the history of the graphic arts as a whole—not just the history of decorating texts—the development that took place in English illumination in the Early Gothic period was of the greatest importance, for it was in the direction of such a development that the future of these arts lay. The illumination in question was in fact a supreme exponent of the style that infused it. Moreover, we find in it the work of craftsmen, who whatever their nationality or training, worked in a fundamentally English mode and are worthy to rank amongst the greatest artists of their day, at times reaching the heights of genius.

[1] Facsimile reproduction: *Psautier de Saint Louis*, Bibliothèque Nationale, Paris, n.d.; Porcher, pl. xliii.

BIBLIOGRAPHY

P. Brieger, *English Art: 1216–1307*, The Oxford History of English Art, Oxford, 1957.

British Museum, *Reproductions from Illuminated Manuscripts*, series i–v, London, 1923–65.

British Museum, *Schools of Illumination*, parts i–iv, London, 1914–22.

S. C. Cockerell, *The Work of W. de Brailes*, Roxburghe Club, Cambridge, 1930.

E. G. Millar, *English Illuminated Manuscripts from the Xth to the XIIIth Century*, Paris and Brussels, 1926.

G. Pollard, 'William de Brailes,' *The Bodleian Library Record*, v, Oxford, 1955, pp. 202–9.

M. Rickert, *Painting in Britain: The Middle Ages*, The Pelican History of Art, London, 1954.

M. Rickert, *La miniatura inglese dal XIII al XV secolo*, Milan, 1961.

O. E. Saunders, *English Illumination*, Florence and Paris, 1928.

G. F. Warner, *Illuminated Manuscripts in the British Museum*, London, 1903.

III. Oscott Psalter, St. John the Evangelist (?) *Circa* 1270

IV. Oscott Psalter, St. Bartholomew. *Circa* 1270

1. Leaf from a Psalter, Christ in Majesty. *Circa* 1220

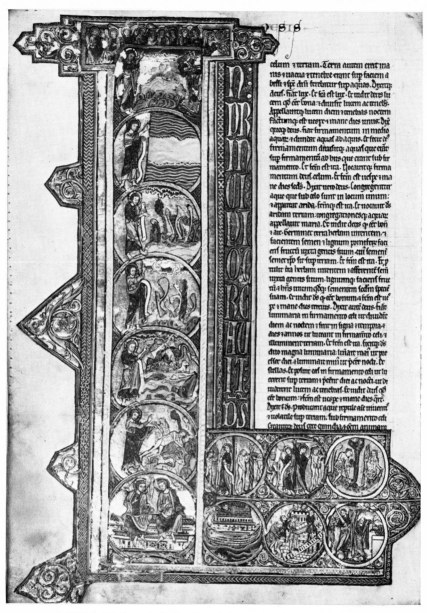

2. Bible of Robert de Bello, Genesis initial. Mid-thirteenth century

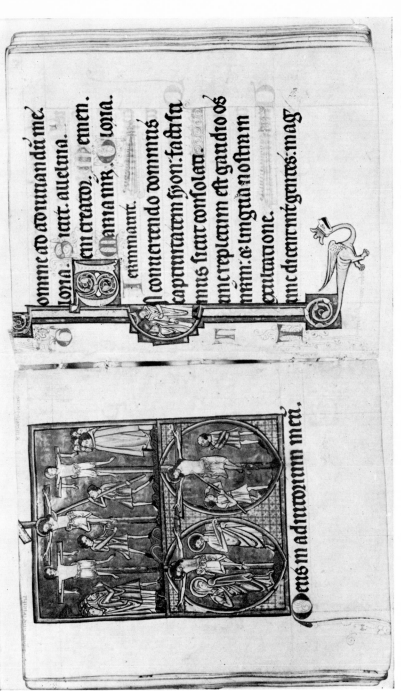

3. De Brailes Hours, on the left: scenes from the Crucifixion; on the right: a scene from the story of the priest suspended from officiating by St. Thomas Becket. Mid-thirteenth century

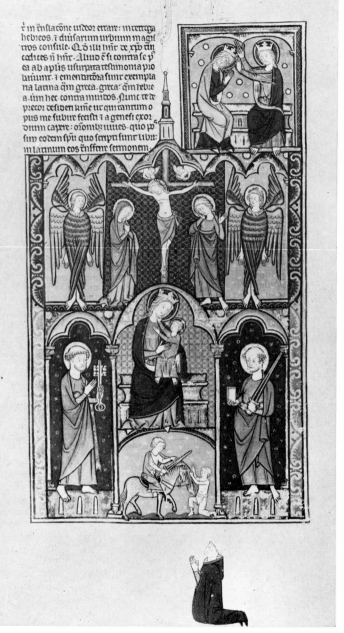

4. Bible of William of Devon, top right: the Coronation of the Virgin; middle: the Crucifixion between seraphim; bottom: the Virgin and Child above, with St. Martin and the beggar below, between Sts. Peter and Paul; in the lower margin: a cleric kneeling. Mid-thirteenth century

O felicia oscula Lactenis labiis impressa. ... inter crebra indicia reptannis inf... ...urgare uer' et te fili' ... alludrer ... neuus et pure def di gemit' imparet...

5. Matthew Paris, Virgin and Child. *Circa* 1240–50

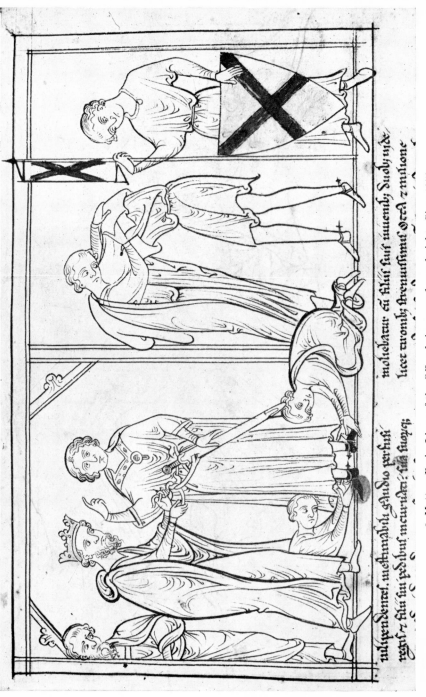

6. Mattew Paris, Lives of the Offas, being armed as a knight. *Circa* 1250

7. Westminster Psalter, St. Christopher. Mid-thirteenth century

8. Brother William, the Apocalyptic Christ. Mid-thirteenth century

9. Trinity Apocalypse, the Adoration of Christ by the Four and Twenty Elders and the Marriage Supper of the Lamb. *Circa* 1245–50

10. Amesbury Psalter, the Crucifixion. Mid-thirteenth century

ꝑ uidet mulierem ebriam de
sanguine sanctoꝛ ⁊ de sanguine martirum ihu· ⁊ miratus sum cum uidissem illam
Admiratione magna· Et dixit michi an-
gelus Quid miraris? Ego dicam tibi sacra-
mentum mulieris ⁊ bestie que poꝛtat eam·
que habet capita vii· ⁊ cornua decem·

P er mulierem babilon designat que
sanguine sanctoꝛ bibitur. Sed ebria cur
idest Ab omni rone speciali alienat· Gria e
nit quia ultio sanguinum sanctoꝛ tra etiam ampl-
iabilem fecerit ⁊ a nna dei alienatur ut non
eet digna quatinus aliquo modo sue saluti po-
set consulere· Et miratus sum in uidissem ⁊ e-
cꝑirantur fideles cum uident replos tantum
A timore dei alienos ut sine aliqua trepidacior
⁊ incrementibꝰ phia mala uigentur⸗ in omibꝰ

flagiciis semetipꝰ demergant scientes deu
nullum scelus impunitum reliqueret uel pꝛe-
sentibus cetisꝙ medicaminibus quibꝰ pꝛe-
sanctus fuerit delentur· Et dixit michi ange-
lus Quare miraris? Eadem significatione hr
bestia in hoc loco quam ⁊ superius dracone dix-
imus habuisse· Significat nanꝗ diabolum
Quid sunt aut capita vii· ⁊ cornua ipm in
sequentibus exponet· Bestia ⁊ diabolus sur au
Aduentum xpi possidens gerens humilitas sta-
est modo· et no posteuit gerens humanis sunt
finnea· quaꝗ xpm Ab electoꝛ coꝛdibus ꝑpuli
sus est· Ascensura uero est de abysso qa xpo
suꝛ xpi soluet sathanas de carcere suo ⁊ er-
bit ⁊ seducet ꝙ sunt sequencia plens mani-
festet· ⁊ in interitum ibit qa cum omnibꝰ re-
gibus quos deceꝑit ⁊ tu omnibꝰ seuellibꝰ
suis eterna pena dampnabit

11. Apocalypse, the Woman drunk with the blood of the Saints. *Circa* 1260–70

12. Abingdon Apocalypse, St. John on the Isle of Patmos. Before 1263

13. Oscott Psalter, upper roundel: the Adoration of Christ by the Magi: lower roundel: the Magi warned by an angel; mid-left: the Creator carrying the sleeping Adam; mid-right: the Creation of Eve. *Circa* 1270

14. Douce Apocalypse, the Rider on the Red Horse. Before 1272

15. Salvin Hours, the Tree of Jesse. *Circa* 1275–80

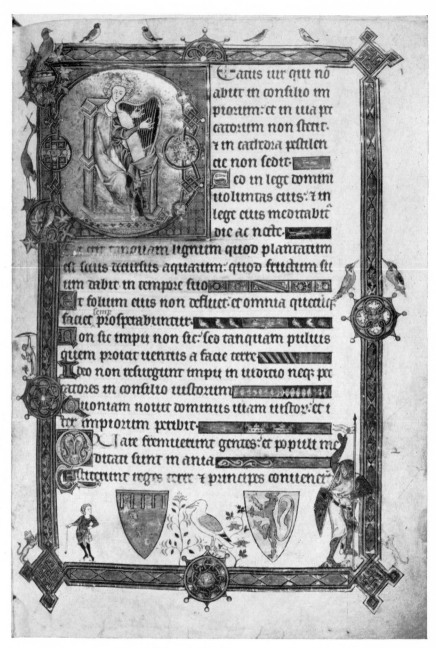

16. Alphonso Psalter, Beatus page. 1281–4